150 MARVEL MOVIE EASTER EGGS

FROM AVENGERS TO X-MEN: 101 MARVEL MOVIE EASTER EGGS

REID GRAVES

The Marvel Cinematic Universe (and affiliated films) have created a unique niche, a sub-genre unto itself in the world of films. And the fans of this genre have shown an uncanny capacity for taking in the smaller details…. a capacity almost as uncanny as that of the Marvel filmmakers to include them in the first place. Most often called an "Easter egg," these details reference things in the comics, the cast and crew and other related films. Collected here are 101 Marvel movie "Easter eggs" for your enjoyment. Next time you watch a Marvel movie, be sure to keep your eye sharp and scanning for both the eggs featured in this book and the ones not yet uncovered.

So turn the page, true believer. Let's get started!

- **Reid**

Iron Man 3 (2013)

Professor Ho Yinsen, the Afghani engineer and scientist who helped Tony Stark escape their cave prison in the first Iron Man, makes a surprise appearance in *Iron Man 3*. He can be seen during the New Years Eve, 1999 flashback that begins the film. This appearance connects back to his dialogue in the first *Iron Man* when Yinsen tells Tony they have already met, despite the latter not remembering it. More importantly, it is here on New Years that Yinsen introduces Tony to Dr. Wu, who would eventually remove both the shrapnel and arc reactor from his chest.

The Incredible Hulk (2008)

Original Hulk television series actor Lou Ferrigno cameos as an easily bribed Culver University security guard in *The Incredible Hulk*. This is actually a repeat of his cameo in the first *Hulk* movie where he appeared alongside Stan Lee. Technically, Ferrigno stands as the only performer to appear in both standalone Hulk movies as the same character. In this film, his enormous muscles prove useless as he is unable to resist the awesome power of Edward Norton's.... pizza.

X-Men: Days of Future Past (2014)

When Quicksilver learns that Magneto can control metal, he comments that his mother used to know someone who could do that. This hints strongly at the comic book origin of Quicksilver being Magneto's son... as does the reaction on Magneto's face. This is further referenced by the name on the mailbox at Quicksilver's home – Maximoff. In the comics, Quicksilver's real name was Peter Maximoff.

X-Men: Days of Future Past (2014)

Another subtle cameo in *Days of Future Past* involved Quicksilver's younger sister, who can be seen in the movie wearing a pink Princess-looking outfit. Being that pink is a shade of red, you might say her costume is scarlet-esque. In the comics, Peter Maximoff's sister is Wanda Maximoff aka the Scarlet Witch, also a child of Magneto's. Director Bryan Singer has since debunked this rumor, but why give Quicksilver a younger sister dressed in pink? Why not a brother or have him as an only child? Sorry, Mr. Singer…. not buying your claim.

Iron Man 2 (2010)

As Tony sifts through his father's belongings, he comes across a brief case. Inside, amid very scientific-looking papers, is an early issue of the Captain America comic. Unbeknownst to audiences at the time, it made good sense that Howard Stark would hang onto such a relic. We would later learn in *Captain America: The First Avenger* that he was friend to Steve Rogers and the two even ran missions together against Hydra.

Multiple Movies

Although Lou Ferrigno has not physically appeared as the Hulk since the string of television movies that followed the original television series, he has continued on in the role... sort of. The ginormous actor's trademark voice can be heard as the character in *The Incredible Hulk, The Avengers* and *Avengers: Age of Ultron*. So whether you realize it not, Ferrigno never really left his most famous role behind.

The Avengers (2012)

While confronting Loki in Stark Tower, Tony says "The Avengers. It's what we call ourselves, sort of like a team. Earth's mightiest heroes." Those last three words comprise the team's long-held slogan in the comics. It might go unnoticed by the average moviegoer, but to hear Robert Downey Jr. say it, it is the kind of moment that gives comic book fans goosebumps. The DC Comics equivalent might be Superman self-referencing himself being faster than a speeding bullet or Batman calling himself the caped crusader. If nothing else, it is a welcome tip of the hat to the core fanbase.

Blade (1998)

Although many consider the first *X-Men* to be the movie that officially kicked off the modern age of Marvel movies, that honor technically goes to 1998's *Blade*. We might more readily group the vampiric vampire-hunter in with the rest of the Marvel gang had the filmmakers not left Executive Producer Stan Lee's cameo on the cutting room floor. While the distinction of Lee's first theatrical Marvel cameo also goes to *X-Men*, it could just as easily have gone to *Blade*. (**Bonus Egg**: Famed vampire Morbius also had an excised cameo!)

Iron Man (2008)

For this egg, refer back to the conclusion of *Iron Man* when Rhodes is standing in Tony's workshop. He turns to the Iron Man suits on display and upon turning back to camera says, "Next time, baby." This was a clear tease of Rhode's becoming War Machine in the sequel. In retrospect, the irony became that Terrance Howard would not return as Rhodes, despite signing up with the clear intention of one day donning the silver suit.

The Avengers (2012)

Built from the battle-damaged remains of Stark Tower, the future Avengers Tower was teased in a blink-and-you'll-miss-it shot from the ending of *Avengers*. As Tony Stark and Pepper Potts overlook plans for the tower's reconstruction, pause the movie (preferably the BluRay version for maximum clarity!) Study the blueprints and you will see plans for individualized living quarters for each member of the team, organized by their respective symbol (Captain America is represented by his shield, Thor by his hammer and so on.)

X-Men 2 (2003)

When Mystique sneaks into Lady Deathstryke's office and logs onto her computer, a long list of familiar mutant names are briefly displayed. If you were to freeze frame on the computer's monitor, you would recognize nearly every name on the list as a current or former X-Men or villain.

A mostly complete list of the mutant identities (and their better known names) appears on the right.

Allerdyce, John (Pyro)
Aquila, Amara (Magma)
Blaire, Alison (Dazzler)
Blevins, Sally (Skids)
Braddock, Elisabeth (Psylocke)
Callasantos, Maria (Feral)
Cassidy (2) (Banshee, Black Tom, Siryn...)
Creed, Victo (Sabretooth)
Dacosta, Roberto (Sunspot)
Dane, Lorna (Polaris)
Drake, Bobby (Iceman)
Dukes, Fred (Blob)
Espinosa, Angelo (Skin)
Gibney, Kyle (Wild Child)
Guthrie, Paige (Husk)
Guthrie, Samuel (Cannonball)
Harada, Keniucho (Silver Samurai)
Kane, Garrison (Weapon X)
LeBeau, Remy (Gambit)
Lensherr, Eric M (Magneto)
Maddicks, Artie (Artie)
Madrox, Jamie (Multiple Man)
Mahn, Xi'an Coy (Karma)
Maximoff (Scarlett Witch and Quicksilver)
McTaggart, Kevin (Proteus)
Moonstar, Danielle (Moonstar)
Munroe, Ororo (Storm)
Omega Red (Russian mutant super soldier)

Iron Man 2 (2010)

In *Iron Man 2*, Tony mocks Senator Stern during the congressional questioning that begins the film by saying "I'm not a joiner, but I'll consider Secretary of Defense if you ask nicely." In the Iron Man comics circa 2003, Tony actually became Secretary of Defense for the United States.

Possible plot point in *Iron Man 4*, anyone?

Captain America: The Winter Soldier (2014)

When Steve Rogers and Natasha Romanoff interrogate SHIELD Agent Jasper Sitwell about his Hydra dealings, they demand to know who exactly the criminal organization is targeting. Sitwell responds, "You! A TV anchor in Cairo, the Undersecretary of Defense, a high school valedictorian in Iowa city. Bruce Banner, Stephen Strange, anyone who's a threat to Hydra! Now or in the future!" Stephen Strange is more commonly known in the Marvel Comics Universe as Dr. Strange, who's been in the running to receive his own feature film for several years now.

X-Men: First Class (2011)

When Mystique attempts to seduce Magneto in bed, he responds "Maybe in a few years," a reference to their future partnership. She then morphs into a slightly older version of herself, though this form is no ordinary blonde bombshell. Mystique's slightly older camouflage is that of actress Rebecca Romijn, who played the character in the first three *X-Men* movies. But this isn't actually her first time out of makeup in the series... recall her being "cured" in *X-Men: The Last Stand*.

The Amazing Spider-Man 2 (2014)

Felicia Hardy, better known in the comics as the secret identity of the Black Cat, appears briefly in The Amazing Spider-man 2. As a young and deranged Harry Osborn demotes Oscorp's topmost executives, he promotes Felicia to a new position overseeing all of them and answering only to him. The character had previously almost appeared in Sam Raimi's Spider-Man 2, only to be written out of the film. She was next included in the shooting script for Spider-man 4, only to have that project cancelled. Her transofmration into the Black Cat has been rumored to feature in a future Spider-man movie.

The Incredible Hulk (2008)

In addition to Tony Stark's surprise visit to General Ross in the film's after-credits scene, there is another, more subtle reference to the greater Marvel Cinematic Universe in *The Incredible Hulk*. In the opening credits sequence, the Stark Industries logo can seen on the schematics for the Sonic Cannon that General Ross hopes to use against the Hulk. **Bonus Egg** – Nick Fury's name also appears on a document glimpsed during the opening credits sequence. Time to pop in the BluRay and get those pause trigger fingers ready!

"LOGAN, MY TOLERANCE FOR YOUR SMOKING IN THE MANSION NOTWITHSTANDING, CONTINUE SMOKING THAT IN HERE, AND YOU'LL SPEND THE REST OF YOUR DAYS UNDER THE BELIEF THAT YOU'RE A SIX-YEAR-OLD GIRL. I'LL HAVE JEAN BRAID YOUR HAIR."

Professor X
X-Men (2000)

Captain America: The First Avenger (2011)

This film contains a quick visual nod to the Human Torch – not the one that Chris Evans played in the Fantastic Four movies, but the original version of the character that debuted in 1939's Marvel Comics #1. Notice the hero's android form inside an oxygen-free glass tube at the Stark Expo early on in the film. As originally depicted in the comics, it was oxygen made the flammable Synthezoid come alive when someone accidentally broke his glassy prison. So technically, had someone only accidentally damaged that case, we could have embarked on an entirely different super hero movie than the terrific one we got.

Iron Man (2008)

The first *Iron Man* features a subtle reference to the title hero's arch-nemesis and the main villain of *Iron Man 3* – the Mandarin. The terrorist organization that kidnaps Tony Stark is known as The Ten Rings. In the comics, the Mandarin draws his power from the ten magical rings he wears. At one point, an image of these ten rings can be behind a captive Tony painted onto a tent wall.

Daredevil (2003)

This easter egg is actually a two-fer. The forensic assistant that shows reporter Ben Urich how Daredevil's cane weapon works is none other than filmmaker Kevin Smith (many of whose films feature Ben Affleck, mind you). Smith is known for writing some of the better Daredevil story arcs of the 1990s comic series. Furthermore, the role he plays is forensic assistant Jack Kirby, named for the famed Marvel Comics artist who drew Daredevil in his earlier days.

The Wolverine (2013)

In a deleted ending to the film, Yukio hands Logan a gift box while on board one of Mariko's company planes. The former X-Man opens it to find a brown pointed mask and yellow-spandex suit that will be awfully familiar to comic book fans. The decision to film this brief nod to the classic Wolverine uniform was not in the original shooting script, but rather an impromptu decision by Director James Mangold. He later trimmed it in the editing room, however, upon realizing that it would not jive with future continuity since Logan would not be wearing the suit in *X:Men: Days of Future Past*.

X-Men Origins: Wolverine (2009)

Despite being featured in early trailers for the spinoff, a cameo by a prominent member of the X-Men team was cut from this film. A very young Storm was originally going to to feature into an early scene when Stryker's mutant team raids a village. The cameo's deletion was announced prior to the film's release and promised to be included on the eventual home video release in order to not disappoint hopeful X-fans.

The Avengers (2012)

Although fleetingly referenced onscreen, the opening scene of The Avengers takes place at the Project PEGASUS headquarters. The acronym stands for Potential Energy Group/Alternate Sources/United States and exists in the comic book universe as a co-venture between SHIELD and NASA to co-investigate things beyond conventional scientific understanding (the tesseract as in this film, for example). Project PEGASUS is also briefly referenced on a crate Tony Stark opens in *Iron Man 2* just before he builds his homemade particle accelerator.

The Incredible Hulk (2008)

In this film, Betty Ross buys Bruce Banner a new set of clothes after a particular hard night of Hulking out. Among her purchases are an elastic-stretch pair of purple sweatpants, a nod to the character's comic book depiction. This is also a practical move on Betty's part to keep Bruce from revealing his "Incredible Bulk" to the world when he eventually Hulks out again.

The Incredible Hulk (2008)

Paul Soles, who voiced Bruce Banner (and Spider-man!) in various cartoons from the 1960s, cameos in this film as Stanley the restaurant owner (Stanley, as in Stan Lee – get it?). It is Stanley who hires Edward Norton's Bruce Banner to deliver pizzas, which he ultimately does to the Culver University security guard played by Lou Ferrigno. So basically, the original Bruce Banner hires the new Bruce Banner to deliver pizzas, which he does to the former Hulk. Follow that okay?

"WHO DO YOU THINK GOD REALLY FAVORS IN THE WEB? THE SPIDER, OR THE FLY?"

Eli Damaskinos
Blade II (2002)

The Amazing Spider-Man 2 (2014)

During the action-packed conclusion of this film, the clock tower is broken during battle and consequently stops ticking at 1:21 AM. In the original run of The Amazing Spider-man comic series, Gwen Stacey dies at the hands of the Green Goblin in issue #121, which served as a major inspiration to this film.

The Avengers (2012)

Look closely at the glass divider separating Tony Stark and Bruce Banner during their conversation aboard the helicarrier. Banner's reflection is not his own, but that of the Hulk.

Captain America: The Winter Soldier (2014)

Refer back to the brief glimpse we get of the Winter Soldier's creation in this film. Can anyone possibly imagine there being a more fitting cameo here than that of comic writer Ed Brubaker? You will recognize him as the bald guy with facial hair and rolled-up sleeves at screen left. He is credited with resurrecting Bucky in the comics and for Bucky's subsequent transformation into the Winter Soldier, making him a very appropriate attendee for the character's onscreen birth.

Thor (2011)

One discrepancy between the comic and film universe mythologies is that in the comics Thor had an alternate ego in the form of medical student Donald Blake. In the film, Thor is banished directly to Earth by Odin in his own body. The film does tip its hat to the comic, however, when Jane Foster gives the Norse God some of her ex-boyfriend's clothes to wear. Later, when she and Erik Selvig attempt to sneak Thor out of the S.H.I.E.L.D. operation in New Mexico, they refer to him as Donald Blake on account of a nametag still left on the clothes.

The Wolverine (2013)

When Logan wakes up in 1973, he does so in an apartment that just so happens to be a shade of yellow not unlike his signature costume. You know, the one we have yet to see him sport on the big screen. Look behind him in and you can catch a nod to the character's previous big screen appearance. The samurai swords that adorn the apartment walls recall his time in Japan for *The Wolverine*.

Iron Man (2008)

In addition to setting up the entire Marvel Cinematic Universe, the original Iron Man contains a short cameo appearance by the first Avenger's signature accessory. An unfinished Captain America shield is visible under Tony's right arm when Pepper walks in on his robot helpers struggling to remove the Iron Man armor. (Tony to Pepper: "Let's face it. This is not the worst thing you've caught me doing.")

"WHO AM I? YOU SURE YOU WANT TO KNOW? THE STORY OF MY LIFE IS NOT FOR THE FAINT OF HEART. IF SOMEBODY SAID IT WAS A HAPPY LITTLE TALE... IF SOMEBODY TOLD YOU I WAS JUST YOUR AVERAGE ORDINARY GUY, NOT A CARE IN THE WORLD...

SOMEBODY LIED."

Peter Parker
Spider-Man (2002)

X-Men: The Last Stand (2006)

The Danger Room scenario that opens this movie features an enormous tease of one of the X-Men's most formidable foes – the Sentinels. Initially visible only in the distance as a pair of glowing eyes…. Logan disappears into the smoke and darkness only to make quick work of the mechanical assassin. Its severed head flies into camera range shortly after. Never you mind the continuity problems this creates when considered alongside *X-Men: Days of Future Past*.

The Avengers (2012)

Look closely at the top left corner of the screen during the ending's television broadcasts, particularly when the waitress is recounting being saved by Captain America. There you will see "A113." This is a popular reference among filmmakers to a classroom the California Institue of the Arts. It first began appearing in Pixar films but has since started popping up elsewhere. More recently, A113 has been seen in films like *Mission Impossible – Ghost Protocol* and *The Hunger Games: Catching Fire*.

The Incredible Hulk (2008)

One unfortunate result of the Hulk franchise lagging behind its Avengers-brethren at the box office is that it has been unable to build upon the villains it sets up. Moments before the battle with Abomination that concludes *The Incredible Hulk*, Tim Blake Nelson's Dr. Samuel Sterns suffers a head injury. Just then - a drop of Banner's gamma-poisoned blood happens to fall onto Sterns' wound, causing his head to pulsate and grow. As Dr. Sterns smiles maniacally, comic book fans everywhere know we are witnessing The Leader being born – famously an arch nemesis to the Hulk.

X-Men 2 (2003)

The scene where Mystique seduces and drugs an unscrupulous guard from Magneto's plastic prison reveals an X-Man cameo. The television playing at the bar shows Dr. Hank McCoy in human form discussing mutants on news program, though the performer is Steve Bacic and not Kelsey Grammar, who would take on the role in the following sequel.

Thor (2011)

While most people recognize Stan Lee's cameo among the rednecks trying to pull Mjolnir out of the ground, fewer recognize comic writer J. Michael Straczynski. He is the unsuccessful chap with the baseball hat and facial hair. Straczynski's work on Marvel's Thor comic was said to have had a strong influence on the direction of the film.

Captain America: The Winter Soldier (2014)

In *Captain America: The Winter Soldier*, Natasha Romanoff's jewelry selection is more than a mere fashion detail. Look closely around her neck to see a necklace with an arrow charm on it – an obvious reference to fellow Avenger Clint Barton aka Hawkeye. As to the true nature and current status of their relationship… we shall look on to *Avengers: Age of Ultron*!

"ALL THOSE YEARS WASTED FIGHTING EACH OTHER, CHARLES... BUT AT LEAST WE GOT A FEW OF THEM BACK."

Magneto
X-Men: Days of Future Past (2014)

Captain America: The Winter Soldier (2014)

The engraving on Col. Nicholas J. Fury's tombstone, while not a Marvel reference, does harken back to what is arguably Samuel L. Jackson's most famous role – that of the bible-quote spewing Jules Winnfield from *Pulp Fiction*. His most famous and oft-quoted verse appears on Fury's grave – "The path of the righteous man…" Look up Exodus 25:17 for the full quote or just watch *Pulp Fiction* if you have not already!

The Amazing Spider-Man (2012)

You would be forgiven for not immediately recognizing the significance of BJ Novak's character in this film on account of his short screen time. But the name Alistair Smythe is one wrought with significance for readers of the Spider-man comics. It remains to be seen whether or not the film universe realizes his destiny in the comics by transforming him into the super villain Spider-Slayer.

The Iron Man trilogy

Although not an overt presence in the Iron Man franchise, the Roxxon Corporation is referenced in all three films of the trilogy. In *Iron Man*, their logo can be seen atop a building during the end fight. In *Iron Man 2*, their logo adorns one of the cars at the Monaco Grand Prix. The conclusion of *Iron Man 3* also takes place aboard an impounded Roxxon oil tanker. In the comics, the corporation is often at odds with Iron Man and are not unlike Oscorp.

Captain America: The First Avenger (2011)

Although Arnim Zola spends the entirety of *Captain America: The First Avenger* in human form rather than his more common robot form, the film does pay tribute to the latter version. The character's face is first seen through the distorted lens of a Hydra labratory magnifying glass, appearing not unlike the gigantic holographic head of his robot suit. Robot Arnim would feature into the next Captain America movie.

The Incredible Hulk (2008)

In *The Incredible Hulk*, General Ross can be seen extracting an experimental super-soldier serum created by Dr. Reinstein marked "Weapons Plus." In the comics, this program was responsible for the creation of numerous super beings including Weapon X.

Thor (2011)

On the outskirts of the small New Mexico film in which the film takes place, there is a tourism billboard that reads "Land of Enchantment – Journey into Mystery." The first part about enchantment is official slogan of New Mexico, but "Journey into Mystery" is the name of the comic in which Thor first appeared in August, 1962 (issue #83).

Captain America: The Winter Soldier (2014)

This film contained another super villain, albeit before his changeover, in SHIELD-agent-turned-secret-Hydra-operative Brock Rumlow. Comic book readers likely know him better as the mercenary that would later assassinate Captain America. At the end of *Winter Soldier*, Rumlow is shown badly injured but still alive – and possibly on the road to becoming Crossbones.

X-Men: Days of Future Past (2014)

Although Stan Lee was mysteriously absent from *X-Men: Days of Future Past*, Wolverine co-creator Len Wein and influential X-Men writer Chris Claremont did put in cameo appearances. You can see them both standing in as congressman at Bolivar Trask's hearing on mutant activity. Claremont also appeared as a neighborhood man mowing his yard in *X-Men: The Last Stand*.

The Avengers (2012)

After Thor takes Loki off the Quintjet down onto the mountain, two ravens fly past them as they converse. Comic book readers (or fans of Norse Mythology) will recognize them as Muninn and Huginn, Odin's pet ravens that often spy and gather information for him. They can also be seen in *Thor* sitting atop Odin's golden throne.

"THEY SAY YOUR WHOLE LIFE FLASHES BEFORE YOUR EYES WHEN YOU DIE. AND IT'S TRUE, EVEN FOR A BLIND MAN."

Matt Murdoch
Daredevil (2003)

Fantastic Four (2005)

In the final scene of this film, the charred and imprisoned Dr. Doom can be seen being boxed up inside of a crate marked for delivery to "Latveria." In the comics, Latveria the fictional country from which Doom hails and over which he exudes his control. In the early days of the Fantastic Four comics, Dr. Doom enjoyed diplomatic immunity from being arrested in other countries due to being the royal monarch of Latveria.

Thor (2011)

In the first *Thor*, the Infinity Gauntlet can be briefly glimpsed inside of Odin's treasure room. Although originally thought to be an insignificant wink toward the fan base, it has become increasingly clear that the Infinity Gauntlet will play a very important role in the Marvel Cinematic Universe. This was never more apparent than during the Collector's exposition in *Guardians of the Galaxy*.

Guardians of the Galaxy (2014)

Humanoid Adam Warlock has a subtle cameo in this film, sort-of. When in need of self-preservation or regeneration, the Marvel super hero retreats into a large cocoon. This cocoon can is clearly visible among the Collector's treasures in both the end-credits scene to *Thor: The Dark World* and in *Guradians of the Galaxy*. Adam's cocoon appears empty amid the scattered remains of the Collector's museum for Guardian's end-credits scene, suggesting he indeed escaped during the infinity stone explosion. Director James Gunn later confirmed that the cocoon was indeed his.

Iron Man (2008)

Listen closely when Tony Stark phones his closest ally during his initial flight test in the suit. Rhodes' ringtone is none other than a MIDI-version of the theme song to the 1966 *Iron Man* cartoon. You know the one… ("Tony Stark makes you feel, he's a cool exec with a heart of steel!") **Bonus Egg** – A swingin' big band version of the cartoon theme song plays when Tony and Rhodes hit the Vegas casino.

Spider-Man 2 (2004)

The scene in which an exhausted Spider-man barely stops a commuter train from running off the tracks (courtesy that dastardly Dock Ock) in this film contains a pair of family member cameos. The two young boys that return Spiderman's mask to him are two of Tobey Maguire's four half-brothers.

The Amazing Spider-Man 2 (2014)

Listen closely when Spider-man answers his cell phone while pursuing the Rhino (in human form) near the beginning of the film. If his ringtone sounds familiar, it is because it is theme to the beloved 1966 cartoon show. As in "Spider-man, Spider-man, does whatever a spider can…"

The Avengers (2012)

The shawarma restaurant seen in the after-credits scene and Iron Man's request to go there may seem completely random at first, but it is not. The same eatery can be seen slightly earlier in the film during the climactic battle scenes. And if you have never tried it, shawarma is *delicious*.

The Amazing Spider-Man 2 (2014)

In *The Amazing Spider-Man 2*, Oscorp is up to some nasty things, even nastier than usual. This is particularly evident when Harry Osborn browses through his company's secret project file directory. References include nods to Venom, Morbius the vampire and Dr. Curt Connors, whom we have already met in all his full scaly glory.

"Ever since that big dude with a hammer fell out of the sky, subtlety's kinda had its day."

Aldrich Killian
Iron Man 3 (2013)

Iron Man (2008)

Although alien-dragon-thing and Iron Man arch-nemesis Fing Fang Foom has not yet appeared in the scaly-flesh in any of the films, he did make a small cameo in the first *Iron Man*. Ready your trigger finger on the pause button during the final fight against Obadiah and you can see a poster of Foom on one of the background buildings.

Guardians of the Galaxy (2014)

The imprisoned spacesuit-wearing-dog seen among the Collector's treasures in *Guardians of the Galaxy* may seem random, but he is actually an obscure character from the Marvel Comics Universe. This is none other than Cosmo, the Russian-astronaut talking dog that heads up the security forces of Knowhere in the comics. In the film, he is played by Director James Gunn's own dog, Dr. Wesley Von Spears.

X-Men: First Class (2011)

During the Cerebro sequence, two familiar faces fly past in the sea of mutants that Professor Xavier encounters. Cyclops appears as a young boy playing with a baseball and glove. Storm also appears as evidenced by her characteristic hair. Neither appear in the film's credits.

The Amazing Spider-Man 2 (2014)

Although Electro's appearance in this film takes inspiration from his re-designed look in the Ultimate Spider-man comic series, there is still a quick nod to the classic green and yellow costume he wore for decades in the comics. The birthday cake Max Dillon makes himself sports green icing and yellow electricity bolts.

The Incredible Hulk (2008)

If you ever saw an episode of *The Incredible Hulk* television series with Bill Bixby and Lou Ferrigno, you likely ended with Bixby's Bruce Banner hitchhiking away to the tune of composer Joe Harnell's "The Lonely Man" theme. That same familiar melody was worked into the score for this film

X-Men: Days of Future Past (2014)

There is a particularly somber moment in this film when it is revealed, or at least inferred, that several members of the "First Class" aren't just absent from this sequel – they did not survive the time between films. When Magneto retrieves his helmet from Bolivar Trask's office vault, Havok's battle-damaged uniform and a clipped wing from Angel Salvadore can be seen on display.

Guardians of the Galaxy (2014)

It would be silly to think that Howard the Duck's cameo in *Guardians of the Galaxy* was news to anyone by now. But it might surprise some, however, to learn that he appears much earlier in the film than the end-credits scene. Scan closely the pods behind the Collector as he roams his museum and you'll see Howard sitting against the glass in one of the cases suspended high above the ground. It is also interesting to note that this is not Howard's first appearance among the Collecto. comr's treasures outside the comics. He also appeared in the same position during an episode of 2013's *Hulk and the Agents of Smash.*

"THAT'S MY SECRET, CAPTAIN.
I'M ALWAYS ANGRY."

Bruce Banner
The Avengers (2012)

Captain America: The First Avenger (2011)

After the opening where Captain America's body is found in the Arctic, we see the Red Skull searching for the tesseract, a lost piece of powerful technology once owned by "the gods". He finds it hidden inside a monastery in Tønsberg, Norway, where the image of a tree is carved. This is no ordinary tree, however, but a reference to Asgard. This is Yggdrasil, which in Norse mythology is the tree from which all life stems from. ("stems" from – get it?)

Iron Man (2008)

As Obadiah Stone watches Rhodes on television, a mighty nice looking chess set sits before him, seemingly in mid-game. Obadiah's comic-self was very fond of chess and was noted for creating "The Chessmen," which was a group of villains whose goal was to attack Iron Man and Stark Industries.

Thor (2011)

Famed comic book writer Walter Simonson can be seen smiling and sitting next to Lady Sif at the Asgardian banquet in this film. One of his key contributions to the Thor universe, Malekith the Accursed, would notably appear in the follow-up, *Thor: The Dark World*.

Iron Man (2008)

The two pilots scrambled to intercept Iron Man during his first flight test are identified as "Whiplash 1" and "Whiplash 2." In the comic books, Whiplash was one of Iron Man's more familiar archenemies. Elements of this character would be incorporated into Ivan Vanko in *Iron Man 2*.

Captain America: The First Avenger (2011)

The campy stage show that Steve Rogers is forced to participate in to raise money for war-bonds in this film features an iconic pose from the comics. The image of Steve punching Hitler memorably featured onto the cover of Captain America #1. (Interestingly, many other super heroes battled Hitler as well. Superman actually choked the bastard.)

The Amazing Spider-Man (2012)

Although most audience members don't pick up on it, there is one performer that appears in both Sam Raimi's *Spider-Man* trilogy and the new *Amazing Spider-Man* film series (forget about Stan Lee for a moment!). Michael Papajohn, whom you will remember as the robber who shot Uncle Ben in Raimi's films, appears as the hapless limo driver shuttling Dr. Ratha around when the Lizard begins his attack on the Williamsburg Bridge in *The Amazing Spider-Man*.

X-Men: Days of Future Past (2014)

When we first meet Jennifer Lawrence's Mystique on the air force base, look closely at the name patch on her military uniform. It says "Sanders" and, apparently being a colonel, that would make her Colonel Sanders… as in the famed founder of Kentucky Fried Chicken. One of the more bizarre Marvel easter eggs, eh?

Spider-Man 2 (2004)

While the Amazing Spider-man comic series has boasted numerous iconic art panels over the years, one in particular is given tribute in Sam Raimi's *Spider-Man 2*. The shot of Peter Parker abandoning his costume in an alleyway trashcan in this film is a direct recreation of a panel from The Amazing Spider-Man #50. It should come as no surprise that the 1967 issue's "Spider-man No More" storyline was a strong influence on the direction of the sequel.

"DO YOU REALLY THINK FATE TURNED US INTO GODS SO WE COULD REFUSE THESE GIFTS?"

Victor Von Doom
Fantastic Four (2005)

Captain America: The First Avenger (2011)

One question that surrounded the first *X-Men* film prior to its release involved how the filmmakers were going to adapt the character's costumes, particularly some of the more colorful ones. Director Bryan Singer poked fun at the costuming dilemma when Wolverine complains, "You actually go outside in these things?" Cyclops then retorts "Well, what would you prefer? Yellow spandex?" Seven films later and we still have not seen Wolverine suit up in his classic yellow yet!

Fantastic Four (2005)

Up until the mid-nineties, Ben Grimm was noted for enjoying the occasional (okay, fairly frequent) cigar not unlike Wolverine. He does not smoke in the film, however, and mentions having recently quit. This is a nod both to Marvel editor-in-chief Joe Quesada's ban on smoking in in the comics and to the fact that *Fantastic Four* was aimed at a family audience and 20th Century Fox did not want to encourage young smokers.

Daredevil (2003)

The boxer that Jack Murdock was told to dive against was named John Romita, a nod to the influential father-son comic book artist duo of Johnny Romita and John Romita Jr. The younger Romita is widely considered to have provided some of the character's most striking and defining images.

Daredevil (2003)

An uncredited Kane Hodder appears in this film as the bodyguard that kills Jack Murdock. Although it's difficult to make out his identity in the actual kill scene, Hodder can be more clearly spotted earlier in the film sitting ringside among Fallon's men. The stunt coordinator and performer is better known to movie fans as the gent who played *Friday the 13th*'s Jason Voorhees the most times (four for those of you counting!).

Iron Man (2013)

The United States President in this film is President Ellis, named so for comic book writer Warren Ellis whose "Extermis" storyline was a primary influence for this film. Ellis also receives a "Special Thanks" in the end credits scroll.

Daredevil (2003)

Daredevil is truly one of those superhero movies that feels a healthy need to pay respect to the writers and artists that evolved the character in the comics. In this film, the names Miller, Mack and Bendis are mentioned as being opponents Jack Murdoch previously won against in the ring. In reality, these names refer to writer/arist Frank Miller, artist David Mack and writer Brian Bendis.

The Amazing Spider-Man 2 (2014)

Although it is only briefly featured in the film, don't let the significance of the Ravencroft Institute be lost on you. In the comics universe, Ravencroft housed some of the most deranged and dangerous Spider-man villains. Considering that the films have Oscorp working in tandem with Ravencroft, there is no telling who else we might see wind up here besides just Electro and Lizard.

"THIS IS SO UNLIKE YOU, BROTHER. SO... CLANDESTINE. ARE YOU SURE YOU WOULDN'T RATHER PUNCH YOUR WAY OUT?"

Loki
Thor: The Dark World (2013)

Iron Man 3 (2013)

This is particularly evident on the BluRay edition of the film, but notice where Taggert sits down outside Graumann's Chinese Theatre. He is actually sitting right next to Robert Downey Jr's cement handprints, which were immortalized there following his success in the original *Iron Man*.

Captain America: The Winter Soldier (2014)

The Walt Disney company is known for localizing its television and movie properties around the world depending on the market and made no exceptions for this film. The pocket notebook list of 21st Century things that Steve Rogers keeps updating for himself to check out is different from country to country. The United State's list includes *I Love Lucy* and the moon landing while the United Kingdom's version includes The Beatles and the 1966 World Cup Final. There are more than a dozen variations on this notebook page.

The Incredible Hulk (2008)

Don't let Ty Burrell's lack of screen time in this film fool you as to his role's importance. His character is credited as being psychiatrist Doc Samson, a well-known character in the comic books and a vital part of the Hulk mythology. It was in the comics that he briefly cured the Hulk, instead transferring the gamma powers, however briefly, onto himself.

Iron Man 2 (2010)

The end scene where Nick Fury discusses the Avengers Initiative with Tony Stark is chock full of Marvel Cinematic Universe references, but one in particular stands out to me as most interesting. It had been confirmed by director John Favreau that one of the dots on the world map behind Fury/Stark indeed pinpoints Africa – more specifically the home nation to the Black Panther!

The Amazing Spider-Man 2 (2014)

Although this detail might have passed you by on the big screen, it is much easier to catch on home video. Look closely when Spider-man humiliates Aleksei Sytsevich by pantsing him in public. The Russian gangster's boxers feature little Rhino's, a nod toward his future identity.

Iron Man 3 (2013)

As Happy Hogan walks through the Stark Industries building stopping people for not wearing their name badges, he looks off-screen and tells someone named Bambi to wear their badge as well. In the comics, Bambi Arbogast was Pepper Pott's secretary. She also briefly appeared in the previous film played by Margy Moore.

Spider-Man (2002)

Although not particularly known as a master of the subtle, director Sam Raimi does pull a clever costuming gag in his first *Spider-Man* film. Notice Peter Parker and Norman Osborn's wardrobe picks during the Thanksgiving meal scene. They are actually wearing each other's colors – Peter in green and Norman in red/ blue. This is appropriate since this encounter is when the two first realize who the other one *really* is.

The Incredible Hulk (2008)

After the Hulk's episode at Culver University, two college students are seen being interviewed by local news. They are named as being Jack McGee and Jim Wilson. Jack McGee was a tabloid reporter who attempted to track down the Hulk in The Incredible Hulk television series, and in the comics Jim Wilson was a young orphan who befriended the Hulk.

Thor (2011)

In this film, when Dr. Selvig mentions he knew a "scientist, a pioneer in gamma radiation" who "wasn't heard from again" after S.H.I.E.L.D. showed up, he's referring to Dr. Bruce Banner, better known as Hulk. Selvig and Banner being colleagues is strictly a creation of the movie universe, as Selvig had not previously existed in the comics.

"I'M GONNA NEED A RAIN CHECK ON THAT DANCE."

Steve Rogers
Captain America: The First Avenger (2013)

Iron Man (2008)

The terrorist known as Raza in this film has very little in common with his comic book counterpart beyond their shared facial disfigurement. In the comics, Raza is not a terrorist, much less an outright villain. He is, however, an alien cyborg who is a member of the space pirate gang known as the Starjammers

X-Men (2000)

Masters of the Universe director Gary Goddard cameos as one of the beach-goers that watch in horror as Senator Kelly emerges from the ocean as a blobby mess. Director Bryan Singer considered Goddard a mentor and sought his advice on directing his first comic book movie.

Spider-Man (2002)

Nicholas Hammon, better known as the first live-action performer to play Peter Parker/Spider-man on the short-lived 1977 television series, can be seen among the scrambling victims during the Green Goblin's assault on the World Unity Festival.

The Incredible Hulk (2008)

Alright sharp-eyed true believers, take note of this film's opening credit sequence. A list of Bruce Banner's associates flashes onscreen and among the list is someone named Rick Jones. In the comic books, it was Jones who originally drove out onto the gamma testing site as a dare. Banner chased after and managed to save him at the cost of becoming the Hulk due to his own gamma exposure.

Iron Man 3 (2013)

You really have to hand it to whoever came up with Trevor Slattery's tattoos. They are numerous, kind of creepy and seemingly unrelated. One tattoo on the actor's neck, however, stands out more than the rest – it is none other than Captain America's shield!

Iron Man 3 (2013)

The character of Brandt in this film is based on Ellen Brandt, who in the comics is the treacherous wife of Ted Sallis, better known as the super hero Man Thing. Oddly, this is Brandt's first appearance in a Marvel movie despite their already being a *Man Thing* film.

(That movie, if you have not seen it, makes several huge departures from the comic and is generally considered a steaming pile.)

Spider-Man 2 (2004)

The "Importance of Being Earnest" posters that adorn the theater where Mary Jane is performing feature a pull-quote that reads: "J. Frazier is especially effective!" John Frazier was the special effects director on this film.

Iron Man (2008)

In this film's theatrical edition, the newspaper that Tony Stark reads in the final scene contains a spy photo snapped from the set of Robert Downey Jr. in costume. Paparazzi photographer Ronnie Adams later sued Paramount Pictures for the unauthorized use of this photo, leading to the studio swapping out the image for a different one on Iron Man's home video editions.

Spider-Man 2 (2004)

Although astronaut John Jameson appears as Mary Jane's fiancée in *Spider-Man 2*, he does not seem to mirror his comic book self. In that universe, Jameson is responsible for bringing the alien symbiote to Earth and becomes the villain Man-Wolf. In *Spider-Man 3*, the symbiote arrives in a different fashion and Jameson's whereabouts are not mentioned.

"WE ARE GROOT."

Groot
Guardians of the Galaxy (2014)

Spider-Man (2002)

In trying to devise a costumed disguise in this film, Peter Parker sketches several outfits he ultimately throws away. One of these sketches is an outright depiction of Marvel Comics superhero Stingray. The page on which Peter draws Stingray contains the note "Biology lecture – bring notes to second peiord!"

Spider-Man (2002)

A fleeting reference is made to anti-hero Venom in the first *Spider-Man* movie. During a meeting at the Daily Bugle, editor-in-chief J. Jonah Jameson demands a photo of Spider-man to which his subordinates claim "Eddie's been trying to get a picture of him for weeks!" This is a reference to Eddie Brock, who would later feature into *Spider-Man 3* along with the alien goo that made him into Venom.

X-Men: First Class (2011)

If the two former Nazi's that Magneto kills look familiar, it's because you might have seen performers Ludger Pistor and Wilfried Hochholdinger also playing Nazi's opposite Michael Fassbender in Quentin Tarantino's Inglorious Basterds.

The Spider-Man trilogy

As is typical with the filmmaker, Sam Raimi's own personal 1973 Oldsmobile Delta 88 can be seen in all three of his *Spider-Man* directorial efforts as Uncle Ben's car. The tradition began all the way back in 1981 with *Evil Dead* and has continued through the years with most of Raimi's works.

Spider-Man (2002)

Xena: Warrior Princess actress Lucy Lawless has a cameo in the first *Spider-Man* movie as a red-haired street punk commenting on old webhead. This should come as no surprise to anyone as Lawless is most famous for her appearance as the title warrior princess in the Sam Raimi-produced television series.

Spider-Man 2 (2004)

Refer back to the operating room scene shortly after Otto's accident in this film. The point-of-view shot from the attacking tentacle will be familiar to horror movie fans for it heavily recalls a similar point-of-view shot often used in Sam Raimi's *Evil Dead* trilogy.